imposter syndrome workbook:

REMOVING THE MASK OF SELF DOUBT

All rights reserved.
No part of this book may be reproduced in any form
without written permission of the copyright owners.
Copyright © 2023 Laura Laine

table of contents

WHAT IS IT?

TYPES

HOW TO USE THIS WORKBOOK

THE IMPOSTER CYCLE

HOW TO HELP

SIGNS & SYMPTOMS

HOPES FOR THIS JOURNEY

VIZUALIZATION

LIMITING BELIEFS

MAY SOUND LIKE

STOP COMPARISON

MY SUPPORT SYSTEM

GOALS JOURNAL

FEARS

SELF ESTEEM BOOST

EVIDENCE OF BEING GOOD ENOUGH

TRIGGERS

WORRY JOURNAL

HYPE LIST

STRENGTHS & WEAKNESSES

ACCEPTING FAILURE

CELEBRATE SUCCESS

AFFIRMATIONS

7 DAY CHALLENGE

DAILY CHECK IN

IMPOSTER SYNDROME HACKS

IMPOSTER JOURNAL

HABIT TRACKER

JOURNAL PAGES

LETTER TO MYSELF

REFLECTIONS

NOTES

what is it?

IMPOSTER SYNDROME IS A UNDERLYING FEELING OF BEING A FRAUD, OVERLOOKING YOUR OWN SKILLS AND ACHIEVEMENTS AND INSTEAD WAITING TO BE "CAUGHT OUT" AS AN UNDESERVING INDIVIDUAL.

THIS FEELING CAN RESULT IN A PERSON WORKING EVEN HARDER TO COMPENSATE FOR THEIR APPARENT SHORTCOMINGS, WHICH IS RARELY AN ENJOYABLE EXPERIENCE AND CAN RESULT IN BURNOUT.

INTROSPECTION AND SELF COMPASSION IS A MUCH KINDER AND MORE EFFECTIVE MEANS TO ACHIEVEMENT. DITCHING IMPOSTER SYNDROME AND REALISING HOW CAPABLE YOU REALLY ARE IS A POWERFUL ACT OF SELF COMPASSION.

types

THERE ARE MANY FACES TO THE IMPOSTER WHICH CAN BE HELPFUL TO BE AWARE OF WHEN ATTEMPTING TO PUT A STOP TO NEGATIVE AUTOMATIC THOUGHTS.

- **THE NATURAL GENIUS:** NEEDS TO BE GOOD AT EVERYTHING THEY PUT THEIR HAND TO. INFLEXIBLE. SUCCESS FOCUSED. PRONE TO COMPARISON.

- **THE SOLOIST:** WILL ONLY WORK ALONE AND AVOID REACHING OUT FOR SUPPORT. OVERLY INDEPENDENT. DOES NOT LIKE WORKING IN TEAMS.

- **THE EXPERT:** ALWAYS OVERLY PREPARED. PEOPLE PLEASER. FEAR OF UNDERACHIEVING. VALUES KNOWLEDGE OVER EVERYTHING.

- **THE SUPERHERO:** TRIES TO DO EVERYTHING, WORKAHOLIC, TOO DRIVEN. TAKES ON TOO MUCH RESPONSIBILITY. NEEDS TO BE NEEDED. JUGGLES TOO MUCH, LEADING TO BURNOUT. NEGLECTS SELF CARE AND THEIR OWN NEEDS AND REST.

- **THE PERFECTIONIST:** HAS IMPOSSIBLY HIGH STANDARDS THAT CAN RARELY BE REACHED. NEVER FEELS GOOD ENOUGH. OVERLY CRITICAL OF THEMSELVES. FEAR OF FAILURE.

how to use this workbook

- UNDERSTAND WHAT IT IS AND WHY IT IS HAPPENING, REMOVE THE FEELINGS OF INADEQUACY, IDENTIFY FEARS AND LIMITING BELIEFS

- PRACTICE SELF COMPASSION IN THE FORM OF AFFIRMATIONS, JOURNAL TO ACHIEVE CLARITY, CHECK IN WITH OURSELVES REGULARLY AND TRACK PROGRESS

- MOVE FORWARD BY CELEBRATING EVERY SUCCESS AND ACHIEVEMENT, ACCEPT MISTAKES AS PART OF LIFE AND LEARN TO BE OUR OWN BIGGEST CHEERLEADER

- INTRODUCE SELF CARE HABITS

- REFLECT AND GROW

the imposter cycle

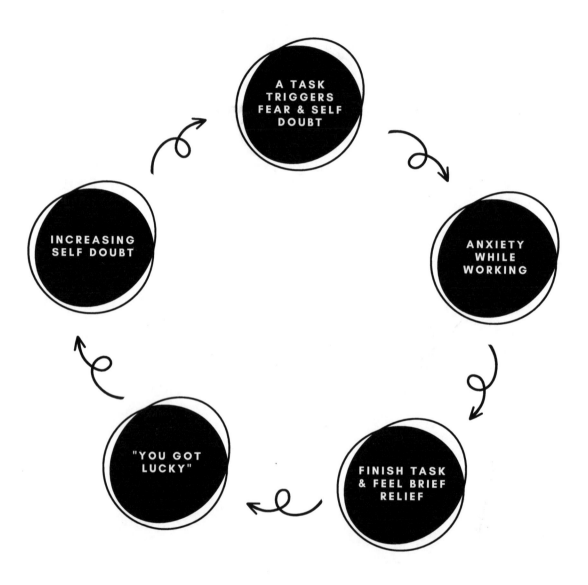

how to help

LEARN THE SIGNS

AFFIRMATIONS

SELF COMPASSION

SHARE YOUR FEELINGS

ACCEPT PRAISE

CELEBRATE SUCCESS

also

- FIND WAYS TO HELP OTHERS TO BOOST SELF ESTEEM AND TURN YOUR FOCUS OUTWARDS
- ESTABLISH A MANTRA THAT SPEAKS TO YOU AND HELPS IN TOUCH-AND-GO SITUATIONS
- PRACTICE HUMILITY AND BE OPEN TO LEARNING AND GROWING

signs & symptoms

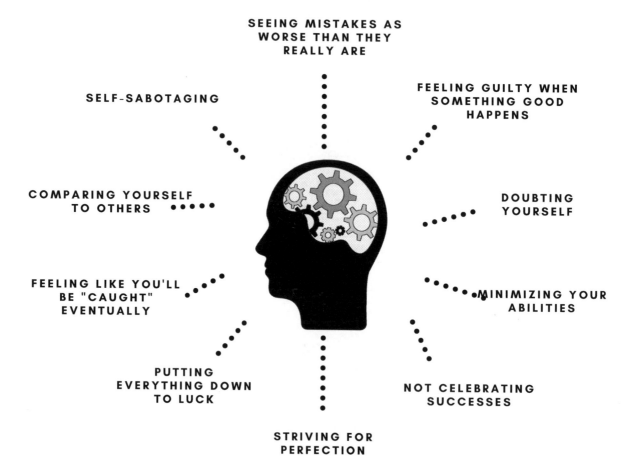

hopes for this journey?

IMPOSTER SYNDROME ROBS US OF THE OPPORTUNITY TO MOVE TOWARDS OUR GOALS AND IDEAL LIFE BUT THAT CYCLE CAN BE BROKEN WITH A LITTLE INTROSPECTION AND SELF FORGIVENESS

HOW DOES IMPOSTER SYNDROME MAKE ME FEEL?

CAN I BEGIN O UNDERSTAND HOW IT BEGAN AND AND FORGIVE MYSELF?

CAN I IMAGINE A LIFE WHERE I DON'T NEED THIS MINDSET ANY LONGER? WHAT WOULD THAT LOOK LIKE AND HOW WOULD I SPEND MY TIME?

I THANK MY PAST SELF FOR TRYING SO HARD UNTIL NOW BECAUSE...

I FORGIVE MYSELF FOR... AND GIVE MYSELF PERMISSION TO...

visualization

USE THIS PAGE TO VISUALIZE THE NEW MINDSET YOU'D IDEALLY LIKE TO APPLY IN EACH AREA OF LIFE, AND WHAT THAT WOULD LOOK LIKE

HOW WOULD MY RELATIONSHIPS LOOK?

HOW WOULD I SPEAK TO MYSELF?

WHAT KIND OF LANGUAGE WOULD I USE?

HOW WOULD MY SCHEDULE LOOK?

HOW WOULD I LIKE TO FEEL IN MYSELF?

WHAT WOULD MY SELF CARE ROUTINE ENTAIL?

visualization

WHAT WOULD CHANGE IN WORK OR SCHOOL?

WHAT WOULD CHANGE IN MY RELATIONSHIPS?

WHAT WORDS WOULD I CUT OUT?

HOW WOULD I ASK FOR HELP AND SUPPORT?

HOW WOULD I CELEBRATE MY ACHIEVEMENTS?

WHAT WORDS DESCRIBE HOW I'D IDEALLY LIKE TO FEEL?

limiting beliefs

FALSE LIMITING BELIEFS ROB US OF THE OPPORTUNITY TO MOVE TOWARDS
OUR IDEAL LIFE BUT THAT CYCLE CAN BE BROKEN WITH A LITTLE
INTROSPECTION AND SELF FORGIVENESS

IN WHAT AREA OF LIFE DO I FEEL STUCK DUE TO LIMITING BELIEFS?

WHAT EXPERIENCES/SITUATIONS HAVE LED TO THIS?

WHAT LIMITING BELIEFS DO I HAVE IN THIS AREA?

I THANK THESE BELIEFS FOR PROTECTING ME BECAUSE...

I FORGIVE MYSELF FOR... AND GIVE MYSELF PERMISSION TO...

limiting beliefs

SOME COMMON FALSE BELIEFS THAT ARE DAMAGING AND HOW TO REFRAME THEM AS EMPOWERING BELIEFS

I'M NOT GOOD ENOUGH	I'M MORE THAN ENOUGH
I AM A VICTIM OF MY CIRCUMSTANCES	I CAN OVERCOME ANYTHING
I DON'T DESERVE TO BE HAPPY	I AM WORTHY OF HAPPINESS
I LIVE IN SCARCITY	I LIVE IN ABUNDANCE
OBSTACLES ARE HOLDING ME BACK	THEY ARE HELPING ME TO GROW
LIFE HAPPENS TO ME	LIFE HAPPENS FOR ME

shift your mindset

NOTE BELIEFS OF YOUR OWN THAT COME UP AND HOW YOU CAN REFRAME THEM

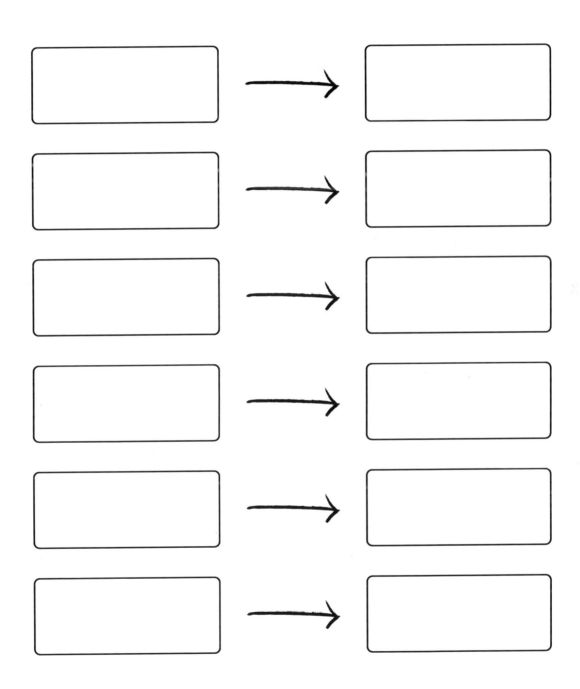

may sound like

YOU'RE NOT QUALIFIED FOR THIS

YOU GOT LUCKY

YOU DON'T KNOW WHAT YOU'RE DOING

YOU NEED TO OVERPREPARE

THEY'LL FIND OUT

HOW DID YOU EVEN GET THIS POSITION?

YOU DON'T BELONG HERE

YOU'RE A FRAUD

THAT'S NOT GOOD ENOUGH

THAT MISTAKE WAS SO BAD

THIS WON'T LAST

SOMEONE ELSE CAN DO IT BETTER

stop comparision

COMPARISON IS THE THIEF OF JOY AND DREAMS AND DISTRACTS US FROM OUR PURPOSE. WE CAN LEARN TO ELIMINATE SELF-COMPARISON AND LIVE IN OUR OWN STORY

IN WHAT WAYS DO I COMPARE MYSELF AND MY LIFE TO OTHERS?

HOW DOES THIS IMPACT MY CONFIDENCE AND SELF IMAGE?

HOW CAN I BREAK OUT OF THIS TRAP OF COMPARISON? (LEARN YOUR TRIGGERS, PRACTICE SELF CARE, LIMIT SOCIAL MEDIA, PRACTICE GRATITUDE, MAKE PEACE WITH IMPERFECTION, FOCUS ON YOUR JOURNEY, EMPOWER OTHERS RATHER THAN JUDGE)?

WRITE SOME AFFIRMATIONS OR MANTRAS THAT MAKE YOU FEEL EMPOWERED TO FOCUS ON YOUR OWN SELF AND YOUR JOURNEY RATHER THAN COMPARING TO OTHERS:

my support system

WE ALL NEED SOMEONE TO RELY ON IN DIFFICULT TIMES. USE THIS PAGE TO IDENTIFY THOSE PEOPLE AND EXPRESS GRATITUDE FOR THEM.

WHO CAN I CALL ON IN TIMES OF NEED?

WAYS IN WHICH THEY SUPPORT ME:

THEY ADD VALUE TO MY LIFE BY...

I ADD VALUE TO THEIR LIFE BY...

WHY I AM GRATEFUL FOR MY SUPPORT SYSTEM:

goals journal

NOW LIST SOME FUTURE GOALS THAT I CAN LOOK FORWARD TO ACHIEVING
AND GET EXCITED ABOUT ONCE I FREE UP TIME PREVIOUSLY SPENT
OVERTHINKING AND BEING TOO HARD ON MYSELF

SHORT TERM GOAL:

THINGS I CAN DO TO REACH MY GOAL:

SHORT TERM GOAL:

THINGS I CAN DO TO REACH MY GOAL:

SHORT TERM GOAL:

THINGS I CAN DO TO REACH MY GOAL:

goals journal

SHORT TERM GOAL:

THINGS I CAN DO TO REACH MY GOAL:

SHORT TERM GOAL:

THINGS I CAN DO TO REACH MY GOAL:

SHORT TERM GOAL:

THINGS I CAN DO TO REACH MY GOAL:

fears

IMPOSTER SYNDROME OFTEN COMES WITH AN INTENSE FEAR OF FAILURE. WHEN WE REDUCE THIS HABIT, WE MAY BE FACED WITH FEARS THAT WE HAVE BEEN AVOIDING. BY GENTLY FACING AND CHALLENGING THESE FEARS, WE CAN MAKE THEM SMALLER.

FEAR:	IS IT REALLY TRUE OR HELPFUL?	CONCLUSION:
I AM NOT QUALIFIED FOR MY JOB. I WON'T LAST.	I WENT THROUGH THE SAME PROCESS AS EVERYBODY ELSE AND PRODUCE RESULTS AS NEEDED.	I DON'T HAVE TO BELIEVE THIS FEAR
FEAR:	IS IT REALLY TRUE OR HELPFUL?	CONCLUSION:
FEAR:	IS IT REALLY TRUE OR HELPFUL?	CONCLUSION:
FEAR:	IS IT REALLY TRUE OR HELPFUL?	CONCLUSION:

fears

FEAR:	IS IT REALLY TRUE OR HELPFUL?	CONCLUSION:
FEAR:	IS IT REALLY TRUE OR HELPFUL?	CONCLUSION:
FEAR:	IS IT REALLY TRUE OR HELPFUL?	CONCLUSION:
FEAR:	IS IT REALLY TRUE OR HELPFUL?	CONCLUSION:
FEAR:	IS IT REALLY TRUE OR HELPFUL?	CONCLUSION:

self esteem boost

LET'S WORK ON BUILDING UP OUR CONFIDENCE AND SELF IMAGE

LIST MY WINS AND ACCOMPLISHEMENTS

A TIME I FELT CONFIDENT AND HOW I MANAGED IT

A MISTAKE AND HOW I TURNED IT INTO A POSITIVE

CREATE MY OWN AFFIRMATION ("I AM...", KEEP IT SHORT, PRESENT TENSE}

NOTES/DOODLES/REFLECTIONS:

evidence of being good enough

FOR 7 DAYS, LOOK FOR AND MAKE A NOTE OF EVIDENCE THAT YOU ARE GOOD ENOUGH, CAPABLE, HELPFUL, ETC AS PROOF OF YOUR SELF WORTH

day 1

day 2

day 3

day 4

day 5

day 6

day 7

RESULTS/NOTES:

triggers

NOTICE ANYTHING THAT TRIGGERS THE NEGATIVE STREAM OF THOUGHTS THAT COME WITH IMPOSTER SYNDROME. THEN THINK OF SOME POSITIVE STRATEGIES OF HOW TO DEAL IN THE FUTURE, SUCH AS HELPFUL DISTRACTIONS, TALKING TO SOMEONE, JOURNALING, ETC.

TRIGGER:	HOW DID IT MAKE ME FEEL?	STRATEGY:
TRIGGER:	HOW DID IT MAKE ME FEEL?	STRATEGY:
TRIGGER:	HOW DID IT MAKE ME FEEL?	STRATEGY:
TRIGGER:	HOW DID IT MAKE ME FEEL?	STRATEGY:

TRIGGER:	HOW DID IT MAKE ME FEEL?	STRATEGY:
TRIGGER:	HOW DID IT MAKE ME FEEL?	STRATEGY:
TRIGGER:	HOW DID IT MAKE ME FEEL?	STRATEGY:
TRIGGER:	HOW DID IT MAKE ME FEEL?	STRATEGY:
TRIGGER:	HOW DID IT MAKE ME FEEL?	STRATEGY:

worry journal

WORKING THROUGH ANYTHING THAT'S ON OUR MINDS BY EITHER LETTING GO OR TAKING BACK CONTROL

A CURRENT WORRY:	SOMETHING I DO ABOUT IT?

A CURRENT WORRY:	SOMETHING I DO ABOUT IT?

A CURRENT WORRY:	SOMETHING I DO ABOUT IT?

worry journal

A CURRENT WORRY:

SOMETHING I DO ABOUT IT?

A CURRENT WORRY:

SOMETHING I DO ABOUT IT?

A CURRENT WORRY:

SOMETHING I DO ABOUT IT?

hype list

MAKE A LIST OF POSITIVE FEEDBACK, BOTH EXTERNAL AND INTERNAL FOR AN INSTANT BOOST IN CONFIDENCE

ACHIEVEMENTS:

COMPLIMENTS RECEIVED:

THANKS RECEIVED:

THINGS I LIKE ABOUT MYSELF:

strengths & weaknesses

UNDERSTANDING WHAT YOU ALREADY DO WELL AND WHERE YOU CAN IMPROVE IS A VALUABLE EXERCISE. REMEMBER THAT NOBODY IS PERFECT AND FINDING ROOM FOR GROWTH IS NORMAL AND POSITIVE.

MY STRENGTHS:

MY WEAKNESSES:

accepting failure

FAILURE IS INEVITABLE, VALUABLE AND A SIGN OF MAKING GREAT EFFORT. THERE IS SO MUCH THAT WE CAN LEARN FROM IT AND CARRY INTO FUTURE ENDEAVORS.

FAILURE/MISSTEP:

WHAT I LEARNED FROM IT:

FAILURE/MISSTEP:

WHAT I LEARNED FROM IT:

FAILURE/MISSTEP:

WHAT I LEARNED FROM IT:

accepting failure

FAILURE/MISSTEP:	WHAT I LEARNED FROM IT:

FAILURE/MISSTEP:	WHAT I LEARNED FROM IT:

FAILURE/MISSTEP:	WHAT I LEARNED FROM IT:

celebrating success

NOW FOR THE FUN PART. MAKE A NOTE OF ANY SUCCESS, NO MATTER HOW SMALL. SOAK IN THE POSITIVE FEELINGS AND OUTLINE WHAT THIS TELLS YOU ABOUT YOURSELF, YOUR SKILLS AND YOUR POTENTIAL

SUCCESS:	WHAT THIS TELLS ME:
SUCCESS:	**WHAT THIS TELLS ME:**
SUCCESS:	**WHAT THIS TELLS ME:**

celebrating success

SUCCESS:	WHAT THIS TELLS ME:

SUCCESS:	WHAT THIS TELLS ME:

SUCCESS:	WHAT THIS TELLS ME:

affirmations

- I AM WORTHY
- I HAVE SO MUCH POTENTIAL
- I DO NOT HAVE TO BE PERFECT
- I AM ON MY OWN UNIQUE PATH IN LIFE
- I TRUST THE TIMING OF MY LIFE
- I DON'T NEED TO KNOW ALL THE ANSWERS
- I DESERVE TO BE HERE JUST AS MUCH AS OTHERS
- I TRUST MYSELF TO MAKE GOOD DECISIONS
- I CAN HANDLE CHALLENGES
- I WILL NOT ALLOW SELF DOUBT TO CONTROL ME
- I AM MORE THAN I HAVE GIVEN MYSELF CREDIT FOR
- I WAS NOT CHOSEN BY ACCIDENT
- I BELONG
- I AM LEARNING AND GROWING CONSTANTLY
- I WILL PUT MYSELF FIRST
- I DON'T WORRY ABOUT THINGS I CAN'T CONTROL
- I'M DOING THE VERY BEST THAT I CAN
- I DON'T NEED TO PROVE MY WORTH
- MY SUCCESS IS NOT DOWN TO LUCK
- GREAT THINGS ARE COMING FOR ME
- ALL OF THE POSITIVE THINGS THAT PEOPLE SAY ABOUT ME ARE TRUE
- I DESERVE HAPPINESS
- I WILL BE AS KIND TO MYSELF AS I AM TO OTHERS
- I AM CAPABLE
- I AM IN A SPACE THAT I DESERVE TO OCCUPY
- I BELIEVE IN MYSELF
- I CAN ENJOY THE PROCESS
- MY VOICE IS WORTHY OF BEING HEARD
- I CAN CONFIDENTLY SAY YES TO OPPORTUNITIES
- MAKING MISTAKES IS NORMAL AND HEALTHY AND DOESN'T MAKE ME ANY LESS WORTHY
- I AM PROUD OF ALL MY HARD WORK
- I AM SAFE
- I DESERVE MY SUCCESSES
- I CAN LET GO OF PERFECTIONISM
- I AM STRONGER THAN I KNOW
- I AM GOOD ENOUGH EXACTLY AS I AM IN THIS MOMENT
- I WILL TRACK AND CELEBRATE MY SUCCESSES, BIG AND SMALL
- I AM COMPETENT
- THE HARDER I WORK, THE LUCKIER I BECOME
- ASKING FOR SUPPORT IS NOT A SIGN OF FAILURE
- IF I MAKE A MISTAKE, I CAN LEARN FROM IT AND COME BACK STRONGER
- MY WORK PROVIDES VALUE TO OTHERS
- I CAN ACHIEVE ANYTHING I SET MY MIND TO
- I AM NOT AN IMPOSTER

my affirmations

MAKE NOTE OF YOUR OWN 10 FAVORITE AFFIRMING STATEMENTS TO REFER TO FOR A BOOST OF INSPIRATION

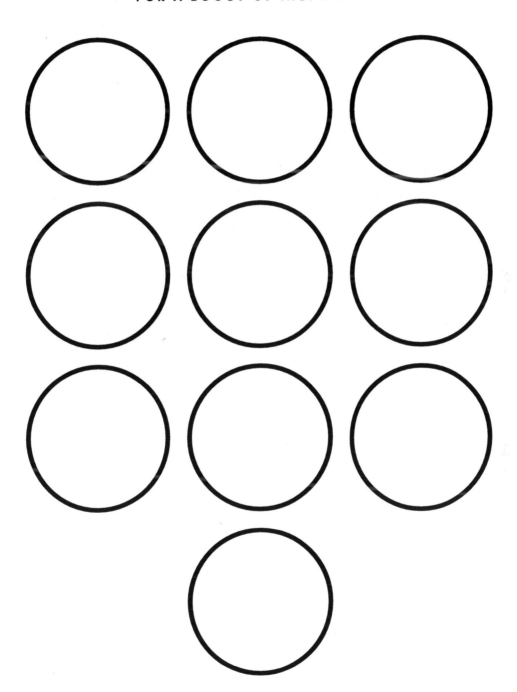

i deserve all of my successes

i don't need to prove my worth

i trust myself

i belong

i don't need to be perfect

i can learn from mistakes

i am not an imposter in any way

7 day challenge

day 1 — LEARN ABOUT IMPOSTER SYNDROME IN ORDER TO IDENTIFY THOSE SNEAKY THOUGHTS

day 2 — USE THE IMPOSTER JOURNAL TO TRACK ANY INSTANCES

day 3 — SPEAK TO A PERSON YOU TRUST ABOUT YOUR JOURNEY AND NEW MINDSET

day 4 — SPEAK AFFIRMATIONS OUT LOUD UPON WAKING TO SET YOURSELF UP FOR THE DAY

day 5 — START A HYPE LIST OF COMPLIMENTS YOU HAVE RECEIVED AND YOUR POSITIVE ATTRIBUTES

day 6 — SAY YES TO YOURSELF TODAY! (TAKE A BREAK, TREAT YOURSELF...)

day 7 — DO SOMETHING TO HELP OTHERS TODAY TO FOCUS OUTWARDS

RESULTS/NOTES:

daily
check-in

M T W T F S S

Date/Time:

What happened today?

Did I have any imposter thoughts?

What small success can I celebrate today?

Affirmation of the day:

Plan for tomorrow:

Today's Mood

Very Happy   Neutral   Very Sad

daily check-in

M T W T F S S

Date/Time:

What happened today?

_____
_____
_____
_____
_____

What small success can I celebrate today?

_____
_____
_____
_____
_____

Did I have any imposter thoughts?

_____
_____
_____
_____
_____

Affirmation of the day:

_____
_____
_____
_____
_____

Plan for tomorrow:

Today's Mood

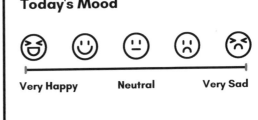

Very Happy　　Neutral　　Very Sad

daily check-in

M T W T F S S

Date/Time:

○○○   ✕

What happened today?

Did I have any imposter thoughts?

What small success can I celebrate today?

Affirmation of the day:

Plan for tomorrow:

Today's Mood

Very Happy   Neutral   Very Sad

daily check-in

M   T   W   T   F   S   S

Date/Time:

○○○   ✕

What happened today?

What small success can I celebrate today?

Did I have any imposter thoughts?

Affirmation of the day:

Plan for tomorrow:

Today's Mood

😆   🙂   😐   🙁   😣

Very Happy   Neutral   Very Sad

daily check-in

M T W T F S S

Date/Time:

What happened today?

What small success can I celebrate today?

Did I have any imposter thoughts?

Affirmation of the day:

Plan for tomorrow:

Today's Mood

Very Happy Neutral Very Sad

daily
check-in

M T W T F S S

Date/Time:

○○○   ✕

What happened today?

Did I have any imposter thoughts?

What small success can I celebrate today?

Affirmation of the day:

Plan for tomorrow:

Today's Mood

😆 🙂 😐 🙁 😫

Very Happy   Neutral   Very Sad

daily check-in

M T W T F S S

Date/Time:

What happened today?

Did I have any imposter thoughts?

What small success can I celebrate today?

Affirmation of the day:

Plan for tomorrow:

Today's Mood

Very Happy   Neutral   Very Sad

daily check-in

M T W T F S S

Date/Time:

What happened today?

What small success can I celebrate today?

Did I have any imposter thoughts?

Affirmation of the day:

Plan for tomorrow:

Today's Mood

Very Happy Neutral Very Sad

daily check-in

M T W T F S S

Date/Time:

What happened today?

What small success can I celebrate today?

Did I have any imposter thoughts?

Affirmation of the day:

Plan for tomorrow:

Today's Mood

Very Happy   Neutral   Very Sad

daily
check-in

M T W T F S S

Date/Time:

What happened today?

Did I have any imposter thoughts?

What small success can I celebrate today?

Affirmation of the day:

Plan for tomorrow:

Today's Mood

Very Happy   Neutral   Very Sad

daily
check-in

M T W T F S S

Date/Time:

○○○   ✕

What happened today?

Did I have any imposter thoughts?

What small success can I celebrate today?

Affirmation of the day:

Plan for tomorrow:

Today's Mood

Very Happy   Neutral   Very Sad

daily check-in

M T W T F S S

Date/Time:

What happened today?

Did I have any imposter thoughts?

What small success can I celebrate today?

Affirmation of the day:

Plan for tomorrow:

Today's Mood

Very Happy   Neutral   Very Sad

daily check-in

M T W T F S S

Date/Time:

What happened today?

Did I have any imposter thoughts?

What small success can I celebrate today?

Affirmation of the day:

Plan for tomorrow:

Today's Mood

Very Happy   Neutral   Very Sad

daily check-in

M T W T F S S

Date/Time:

◯◯◯ ✕

What happened today?

Did I have any imposter thoughts?

What small success can I celebrate today?

Affirmation of the day:

Plan for tomorrow:

Today's Mood

😆 🙂 😐 🙁 😖

Very Happy Neutral Very Sad

daily check-in

M T W T F S S

Date/Time:

What happened today?

Did I have any imposter thoughts?

What small success can I celebrate today?

Affirmation of the day:

Plan for tomorrow:

Today's Mood

Very Happy   Neutral   Very Sad

daily check-in

M T W T F S S

Date/Time:

What happened today?

What small success can I celebrate today?

Did I have any imposter thoughts?

Affirmation of the day:

Plan for tomorrow:

Today's Mood

Very Happy   Neutral   Very Sad

daily check-in

M T W T F S S

Date/Time:

What happened today?

What small success can I celebrate today?

Did I have any imposter thoughts?

Affirmation of the day:

Plan for tomorrow:

Today's Mood

Very Happy   Neutral   Very Sad

daily check-in

M T W T F S S

Date/Time:

What happened today?

What small success can I celebrate today?

Did I have any imposter thoughts?

Affirmation of the day:

Plan for tomorrow:

Today's Mood

Very Happy   Neutral   Very Sad

daily check-in

M T W T F S S

Date/Time:

What happened today?

What small success can I celebrate today?

Did I have any imposter thoughts?

Affirmation of the day:

Plan for tomorrow:

Today's Mood

Very Happy — Neutral — Very Sad

daily check-in

M T W T F S S

Date/Time:

○ ○ ○   ✕

What happened today?

What small success can I celebrate today?

Did I have any imposter thoughts?

Affirmation of the day:

Plan for tomorrow:

Today's Mood

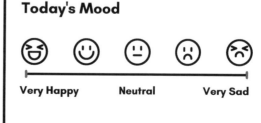

Very Happy   Neutral   Very Sad

imposter syndrome hacks

HELP OTHERS

DO SOMETHING CREATIVE

MINDFULNESS MEDITATION

CONFIDE IN SOMEONE

LEARN SOMETHING NEW

GET SOME FRESH AIR

DO SOMETHING FUN

LIST YOUR ACCOMPLISHMENTS

VISUALIZE SUCCESS

imposter journal:

HOW TO USE

Imposter thought/feeling: what thought crept in to stop us in our tracks and give the feeling of being undeserving/incapable/less than?

Trigger: did something specific trigger this (something someone said, something not going to plan, etc) or was it an automatic habitual thought?

Describe the situation: what was happening at the time? This can be useful in identifying potentially tricky or triggering scenarios. In future, we can prepare ahead of time.

Is the imposter thought true or helpful? If the answer is no, we have full permission to let it go and move forward.

How can I challenge it? Use actual facts as evidence that this thought is untrue and take it's power away.

M T W T F S S

Date:

IMPOSTER JOURNAL

Imposter thought/feeling:

Trigger:

Describe the situation:

Is the imposter thought true or helpful?

How can I challenge it?

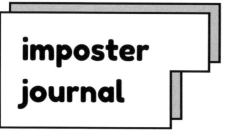

M T W T F S S

Date:

IMPOSTER JOURNAL

Imposter thought/feeling:

Trigger:

Describe the situation:

Is the imposter thought true or helpful?

How can I challenge it?

M T W T F S S

Date:

IMPOSTER JOURNAL

Imposter thought/feeling:

_____
_____
_____
_____

Trigger:

_____
_____

Describe the situation:

_____
_____
_____
_____
_____

Is the imposter thought true or helpful?

_____
_____
_____
_____
_____

How can I challenge it?

_____
_____
_____
_____
_____

M T W T F S S

Date:

IMPOSTER JOURNAL

Imposter thought/feeling:

Trigger:

Describe the situation:

Is the imposter thought true or helpful?

How can I challenge it?

M   T   W   T   F   S   S

Date:

○○○   IMPOSTER JOURNAL   ✕

Imposter thought/feeling:

Trigger:

Describe the situation:

Is the imposter thought true or helpful?

How can I challenge it?

M T W T F S S

Date:

○○○ IMPOSTER JOURNAL ✕

Imposter thought/feeling:

_____
_____
_____
_____

Trigger:

_____
_____

Describe the situation:

_____
_____
_____
_____
_____
_____

Is the imposter thought true or helpful?

_____
_____
_____
_____
_____
_____

How can I challenge it?

_____
_____
_____
_____
_____
_____

M T W T F S S

Date:

IMPOSTER JOURNAL

Imposter thought/feeling:

Trigger:

Describe the situation:

Is the imposter thought true or helpful?

How can I challenge it?

M T W T F S S

Date:

IMPOSTER JOURNAL

Imposter thought/feeling:

Trigger:

Describe the situation:

Is the imposter thought true or helpful?

How can I challenge it?

M T W T F S S

Date:

IMPOSTER JOURNAL

Imposter thought/feeling:
_____
_____
_____

Trigger:
_____
_____

Describe the situation:
_____
_____
_____
_____
_____

Is the imposter thought true or helpful?
_____
_____
_____
_____
_____

How can I challenge it?
_____
_____
_____
_____
_____

M T W T F S S

Date:

IMPOSTER JOURNAL

Imposter thought/feeling:

Trigger:

Describe the situation:

Is the imposter thought true or helpful?

How can I challenge it?

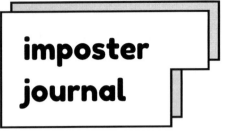

M T W T F S S

Date:

IMPOSTER JOURNAL

Imposter thought/feeling:

Trigger:

Describe the situation:

Is the imposter thought true or helpful?

How can I challenge it?

M T W T F S S

Date:

IMPOSTER JOURNAL

Imposter thought/feeling:
_____
_____
_____
_____

Trigger:
_____
_____

Describe the situation:
_____
_____
_____
_____
_____
_____

Is the imposter thought true or helpful?
_____
_____
_____
_____
_____
_____

How can I challenge it?
_____
_____
_____
_____
_____
_____

habit tracker

USE THIS 30 DAY TRACKER TO BREAK OLD HABITS AND BUILD NEW AND MORE HELPFUL ONES. THIS USEFUL TEMPLATE MAY BE USED FOR ANY OTHER PRODUCTIVE OR SELF CARE HABITS THAT YOU FEEL INSPIRED TO PRACTICE.

START DATE: 1st March

END DATE: 30th March

HABIT: list a small succes every day

X	X	X	4	5	6	7
8	9	10	11	12	13	14
15	16	17	18	19	20	21
22	23	24	25	26	27	28
29	30	31	32	33	34	35
36	37	38	39	40	41	42
43	44	45	46	47	48	49

REASONS: boost self esteem and practice a more positive mindse

EXAMPLE

START DATE: _____   END DATE: _____

HABIT: _____

1	**2**	**3**	**4**	**5**
6	**7**	**8**	**9**	**10**
11	**12**	**13**	**14**	**15**
16	**17**	**18**	**19**	**20**
21	**22**	**23**	**24**	**25**
26	**27**	**28**	**29**	**30**

REASONS:

START DATE: _____   END DATE: _____

HABIT: _____

1	2	3	4	5
6	7	8	9	10
11	12	13	14	15
16	17	18	19	20
21	22	23	24	25
26	27	28	29	30

REASONS:

START DATE: _____ END DATE: _____

HABIT: _____

1	2	3	4	5
6	7	8	9	10
11	12	13	14	15
16	17	18	19	20
21	22	23	24	25
26	27	28	29	30

REASONS:

START DATE: END DATE:

HABIT:

1	2	3	4	5
6	7	8	9	10
11	12	13	14	15
16	17	18	19	20
21	22	23	24	25
26	27	28	29	30

REASONS:

START DATE: _____   END DATE: _____

HABIT: _____

1	**2**	**3**	**4**	**5**
6	**7**	**8**	**9**	**10**
11	**12**	**13**	**14**	**15**
16	**17**	**18**	**19**	**20**
21	**22**	**23**	**24**	**25**
26	**27**	**28**	**29**	**30**

REASONS: _____

START DATE: _____ END DATE: _____

HABIT: _____

1	2	3	4	5
6	7	8	9	10
11	12	13	14	15
16	17	18	19	20
21	22	23	24	25
26	27	28	29	30

REASONS:

journal

DESCRIBE LIVING YOUR IDEAL DAILY LIFE WITHOUT THE BURDEN OF IMPOSTER SYNDROME. WHAT DOES IT LOOK LIKE AND HOW DOES IT FEEL?

journal

MAKE A LIST OF EVERYTHING YOU HAVE TO OFFER:

journal

WHAT GOALS WILL BE POSSIBLE WHEN I AM NOT SABOTAGED BY
IMPOSTER SYNDROME? WHAT PRACTICAL TASKS WILL MAKE
THESE GOALS POSSIBLE?

journal

WHAT PAST BELIEFS/EXPERIENCES DO I BELIEVE LED TO MY SELF DOUBT? RECOGNISE THAT THIS WAS NOT MY FAULT IN ANY WAY, THANK MYSELF FOR COPING IN THE BEST WAY I COULD AND MOVE ON TO A MORE COMPASSIONATE MINDSET.

journal

DESCRIBE MY SUPPORT SYSTEM AND THE WAYS IN WHICH I AM
GRATEFUL FOR THEM

journal

WHAT COMPLIMENTS DO YOU FIND HARD TO ACCEPT? WHY DO YOU THINK THIS IS?

journal

HOW DO YOU THINK IMPOSTER SYNDROME HAS HELD YOU BACK IN THE PAST?

journal

IF I EXPERIENCE A CHALLENGE IN THE NEAR FUTURE, WHAT ARE SOME MORE HELPFUL COPING MECHANISMS THAT I CAN USE?

journal

WHAT PROGRESS HAVE I MADE RECENTLY ON THIS JOURNEY? LIST ANY WINS, BIG OR SMALL.

journal

DESCRIBE SOME OF YOUR BIGGEST GOALS FOR THE FUTURE AND THEIR MEANING TO YOU

journal

WHAT ADVICE WOULD YOU NOW GIVE TO SOMEONE WHO SUFFERS WITH IMPOSTER SYNDROME?

journal

WHAT CAN YOU DO TO BOOST YOUR CONFIDENCE?

letter to myself

WITH LOVE AND COMPASSION, WRITE A LETTER TO YOURSELF. RELEASE ANY GUILT THAT YOU MAY BE HOLDING ONTO.
SOME PROMPTS: I FORGIVE..., FROM NOW ON..., I RELEASE...

reflections

DO I FEEL MORE IN CONTROL OF THE IMPOSTER?

WHAT IS MY NEW FAVORITE ACTIVITY FROM THIS BOOK AND WHY?

WHAT HAS BEEN MY BIGGEST REALIZATION (E.G. A LIMITING BELIEF, FEAR, MEMORY)?

reflections

WHAT PART OF MY FUTURE STORY EXCITES ME MOST?

WHAT IS MY ONE BIGGEST TAKE AWAY FROM THIS EXPERIENCE?

HOW WOULD I LIKE TO MOVE FORWARD ON THIS JOURNEY?

notes

notes

notes

notes

notes

Printed in Great Britain
by Amazon